To My Marvelous Brother:

All boys love Easter
bunnies, chocolate, egg hunts, and
a basket full of wonderful things!

I hope Easter is egg-citing...
filled with fun and adventure for
my MARVELOUS BROTHER!

A boy as special as you
should get your favorite
goodies from the Easter bunny!

Here's wishing the Easter
Bunny brings you the best and
most colorful eggs!

HOP! HOP! HOP! The Easter Bunny is on his way to make sure you have plenty of sweet treats!

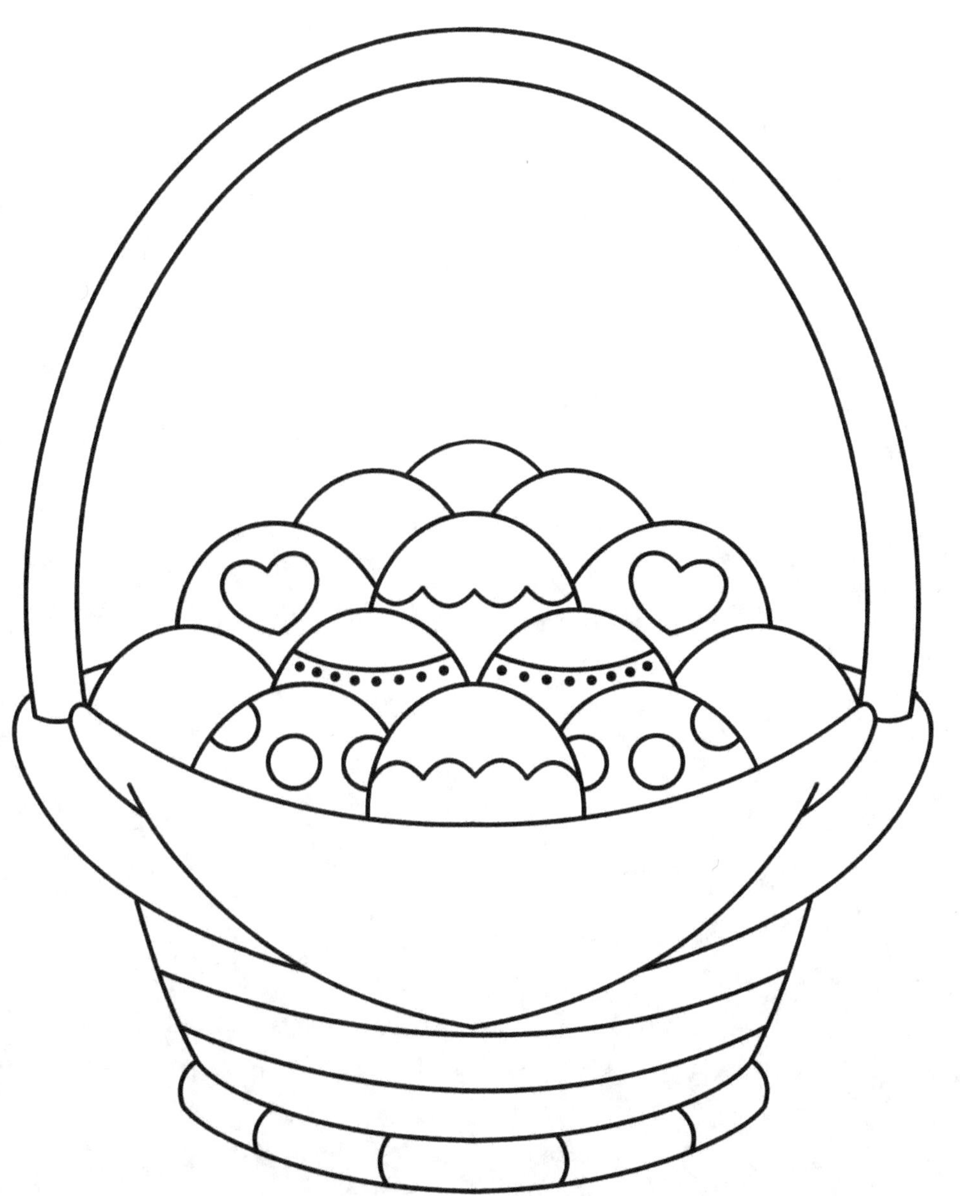

Wishing you a wonderful time as you celebrate Easter with family & friends!

One of the best things about Easter is...
all of the chocolate eggs
boys get to eat!

The Easter Bunny told me that you
are an EGG-STRA
MARVELOUS BROTHER!

There is no other boy in the world that deserves more fun than you this Easter!

Have a fantastic Easter with plenty of chirping chickens & fluffy bunnies!

Good luck this year on your
Easter egg hunt!

Happy Easter
To My MARVELOUS BROTHER!
(Coloring Card)
(Personalized Card) Easter Messages,
Wishes, & Greetings for Children!

May you have a wonderful
holiday and your basket is filled with
lots of holiday things.